CHANGE
PREACHER'S
JOURNAL 4

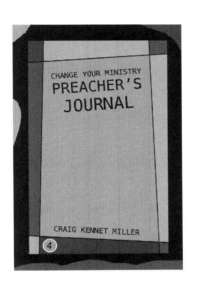

Craig Kennet Miller

changeyourministry.org

The Rev. Dr. Craig Kennet Miller is the founder of Change Your Ministry. He is the former Director of Congregational Development at Discipleship Ministries of the United Methodist Church and the creator of *TeamWorks.* He is the author of numerous books including *Boomer Spirituality: Seven Values for the Second Half of Life, iKids: Parenting in the Digital Age* and *NextChurch.Now.*

Books in the Change Your Ministry series by Craig Kennet Miller can be found on Amazon

Change Your Ministry Leader's Assessment
Change Your Ministry Leader's Assessment Seminar Guidebook
Change Your Ministry Preacher's Journal 1, 2, 3, & 4

You may contact him at cmiller@changeyourministry.org.

WELCOME

The *Change Your Ministry Pastor's Journal 4* is designed to create, organize, and plan your preaching for the next three months. Inside, you will find enough templates for thirteen weeks and dotted pages for jotting down your ideas, developing your sermons, and generating ideas.

There are four journals in the series, with enough templates for three months in each journal. Each journal has its own color and number.

If you want to keep track of what you have created in a digital file, take a picture with your phone and upload it to an app like Google Keep. It's an easy way to save your material and to share with others as needed.

My prayer for you is this journal becomes an invaluable resource filled with the knowledge and inspiration that will lead your congregation into a future filled with the hope and grace of Jesus Christ.

Blessings,
Craig

Table of Contents

WHY PREACH?

Preaching is the means through which God calls a faith community into a blessed future. Consistent preaching by the same pastor over time invites people into a long conversation about how to be a follower of Jesus Christ.

At its very heart, preaching is about creating a relationship with a group of people that brings transformation in their lives. Over time it casts a vision of what God is calling this particular faith community to become.

To be successful, a preacher needs to have a system, a standard way of preparation that builds on past performance and creates forward momentum. The system also needs to have a built-in way to keep the preacher from repeating the same thing over and over again.

Some do this by using the Lectionary. Each week a new set of scriptures are provided which allows sermons to move through the Biblical narrative in an orderly way. Others like to offer a series of messages based on topics like "Love like Jesus" or "Find Your Way Home."

To avoid speaking on the same point every week, a preacher needs a way to check to see they are covering a variety of themes that grows the spiritual life of the church.

THE VALUES INDEX

Your *Change Your Ministry Preacher's Journal* includes the Values Index developed for the *Change Your Ministry Pastor's Assessment*. The index lists six passions (Voice, Assets, Love, Uniqueness, Empowerment, Spirituality) that empower and fuel ministry. Use the index to create sermons that focus on each of these values, so your congregation is given a broader understanding of God's call for their lives.

VALUES INDEX

Voice	Voice is what defines a faith community's beliefs and practices, its understanding of scripture, its call for justice and reconciliation, its denominational affiliation, and the context in which it finds itself.
Assets	The most important asset in a congregation is its people. A vibrant church invests in its people by equipping them for ministry and investing in their spiritual lives. Staffing, finances, and facilities support the ministry of the people.
Love	The people a church loves communicates to the broader community who is welcome to be part of the faith community. Love is defined by who is given permission to be in leadership in worship and its administrative structures.
Uniqueness	Every church is a spiritual alternative in its area. Its uniqueness (worship style, spiritual practices, traditions, missional engagement, and beliefs) invites people to explore their faith in a distinct way.
Empowerment	Transformation happens as a faith community releases its people to be advocates for justice, agents of compassion, and givers of hope to those who feel disconnected from God.
Spirituality	Prayer, scripture reading, worship, small groups, faith-sharing, service with others, and stewardship are ways people grow in faith and practice.

SERMON TRACKER (LAST THREE MONTHS)

Identify the focus of your sermons by shading in the first initial of the Values Index.

Voice	Assets	Love	Uniqueness	Empowerment	Spirituality

DATE	SERMON TITLE	VALUES INDEX
		V A L U E S
		V A L U E S
		V A L U E S
		V A L U E S
		V A L U E S
		V A L U E S
		V A L U E S
		V A L U E S
		V A L U E S
		V A L U E S
		V A L U E S
		V A L U E S
		V A L U E S

SERMON TRACKER (NEXT THREE MONTHS)

Identify the focus of your sermons by shading in the first initial of the Values Index.

Voice	**A**ssets	**L**ove	**U**niqueness	**E**mpowerment	**S**pirituality

DATE	SERMON TITLE	VALUES INDEX
		V A L U E S
		V A L U E S
		V A L U E S
		V A L U E S
		V A L U E S
		V A L U E S
		V A L U E S
		V A L U E S
		V A L U E S
		V A L U E S
		V A L U E S
		V A L U E S
		V A L U E S

THE PREACHING SYSTEM

The Preacher's Journal contains three basic templates, the *Topic Map*, the *Sermon Starter*, and *Three Months From Now*. These are designed to create a pattern for developing your sermons. Included in the journal are four *Topic Maps* for creating series, thirteen *Sermon Starters* for designing sermons, and three *Three Months From Now* for future planning. You can also use the dotted pages facing the *Sermon Starters* to draw a *Topic Map* for that particular message.

THE TOPIC MAP

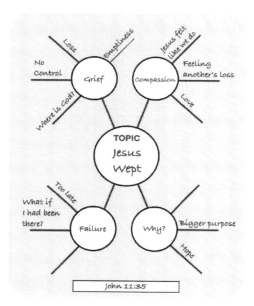

The Topic Map is designed to generate ideas, giving you a pattern to jot down your thoughts as you encounter a topic or theme.

In the center topic circle, write the topic. In our example, we have "Jesus Wept "from John 11:35.

In the other circles, jot down major thoughts that spring from the center. On the lines, jot down additional ideas that expand on the thoughts. You can add lines as needed.

Usually, the circle with the most lines is the idea that has the most energy – the most potent example. You could use this example as a four-part sermon series on grief. With each circle, you could add additional scriptures to expand on the initial thoughts. Or you could use this example for one sermon, with some of the circles highlighting significant points.

SERMON STARTER

Use the categories listed to craft your message. You can be as flexible as you want. Use this to give you a first look at what you are creating. Use the dotted facing page to do a Topic Map or expand your thoughts as needed. Use the Values Index to track your focus.

SERMON STARTER

DATE	March 5th
SEASON/EVENT	Third Sundy of Lent
SCRIPTURE	John 11.35, Revelation 21.4
TITLE/THEME	Compassion - God dries all our tears.
KEY IDEA	Because Jesus experienced grief like us, he offers us hope through his compassion.
ILLUSTRATION	Jesus reaction when he met Mary and saw her pain.
ILLUSTRATION	How its hard to know what to say to someone who has lost a loved one.
CONCLUDING STORY	The great scene in Revelation 21 when God proclaimes a new heaven and earth, when God will wipe away all our tears.
OTHER	Baptism at 10:30 am service (baptism as death of self and new life in Christ). Romans 6.4

VALUES INDEX (circle the values highlighted in this message)

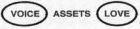 (VOICE) ASSETS (LOVE) UNIQUENESS - EMPOWERMENT - SPIRITUALITY

changeyourministry.org

THREE MONTHS AHEAD

Before starting your next group of sermons, look forward three months ahead to begin your creative process. If you already have it planned, use this to make mid-course corrections. Share with staff and other worship leaders to get their ideas and input.

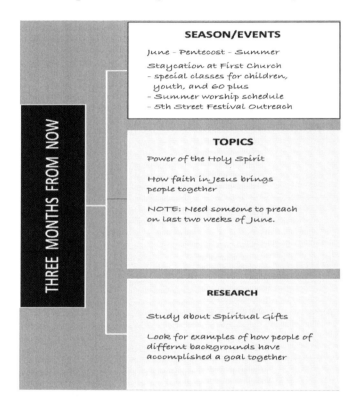

TIME BLOCKING

Use the technique of time blocking to set up your basic weekly schedule. Try to do one or two things during each block. Set aside two full blocks (for example, Tuesday Morning and Thursday afternoon) for sermon and worship preparation. Set aside a minimum of seven blocks for time off and family and personal time. Develop with family and close friends to make sure you have a balanced schedule. Share with staff and church leaders, so they know your schedule.

TIME BLOCKING			
	Morning	Afternoon	Evening
MONDAY			
TUESDAY			
WEDNESDAY			
THURSDAY			
FRIDAY			
SATURDAY			
SUNDAY			

- Sermon Preparation
- Prayer and visioning
- Community Involvement
- Teaching
- Social Media
- Office Hours
- Personal Time (Exercise, etc.)
- Staff meetings

- Worship preparation
- Meetings and leader development
- Caregiving
- Denominational Responsibilities
- Tasks (Nuts & Bolts)
- Time Off
- Personal Relationships
- Family Time

MONTHLY CALENDAR

Set up your monthly calendar by adding the month and year. Refer to a calendar and in the "Days Column" write in the initial of each day (M, T, W, T, F, S, S). Use a different color for Saturday and Sunday. Use this to set up your blocks of time and to keep track of the flow of your work.

MONTH AND YEAR:				
DATE	DAYS	MORNING	AFTERNOON	EVENING
1				
2				
3				
4				
5				
6				
7				
8				
9				
10				
11				
12				
13				
14				
15				
16				
17				
18				
19				
20				
21				
22				
23				
24				
25				
26				
27				
28				
29				
30				
31				

MONTH AND YEAR:				
DATE	DAYS	MORNING	AFTERNOON	EVENING
1				
2				
3				
4				
5				
6				
7				
8				
9				
10				
11				
12				
13				
14				
15				
16				
17				
18				
19				
20				
21				
22				
23				
24				
25				
26				
27				
28				
29				
30				
31				

MONTH AND YEAR:				
DATE	DAYS	MORNING	AFTERNOON	EVENING
1				
2				
3				
4				
5				
6				
7				
8				
9				
10				
11				
12				
13				
14				
15				
16				
17				
18				
19				
20				
21				
22				
23				
24				
25				
26				
27				
28				
29				
30				
31				

SPIRITUAL LIFE QUESTIONS

Identify two spiritual disciplines you will focus on during this quarter. Use this as a way to try different spiritual disciplines and to grow in your own personal spirituality.

SPIRITUAL LIFE QUESTIONS

1. In which spiritual discipline(s) do you want to grow?

Pick one discipline you will try from now until the next time you meet

changeyourministry.org

_ Weekly worship
_ Daily Bible Reading
_ Daily Prayer
_ Frequency of communion
_ Service to others
_ Fasting or abstinence
_ Tithing/Giving
_ Family Prayer
_ Other

SPIRITUAL LIFE QUESTIONS

2. What is your plan for continued spiritual growth and development?

Out of all these choices, pick one discipline you will try from now until the next time you meet

changeyourministry.org

HOW DO YOU CONNECT WITH GOD?
_ Day apart   _ Worship
_ Daily devotion   _ Family prayer
_ Prayer partner or coach   _ Other

HOW ARE YOU CONNECTING WITH OTHERS?
_ Time alone with spouse, partner, or friend
_ Focused time with your children
_ Regular connection with extended family
_ Prayer or accountability group
_ Time with friends outside of church

HOW ARE YOU TAKING CARE OF YOUR BODY?
_ Exercise class   _ Walking/Running
_ Healthy diet   _ Active in a sport
_ Workout at a gym   _ Other

WHAT ARTS FEED YOUR SOUL?
_ Playing a musical instrument   _ Singing
_ Writing   _ Drawing
_ Cooking   _ Other

---

1. _____

2. _____

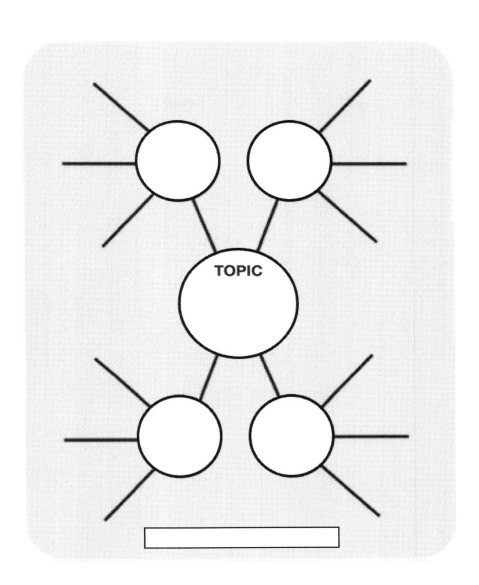

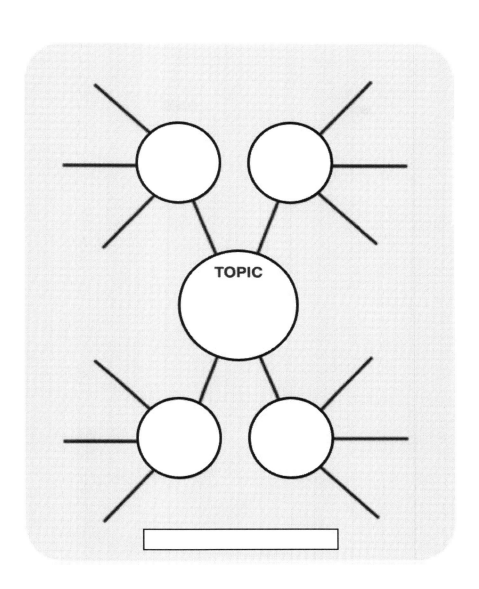

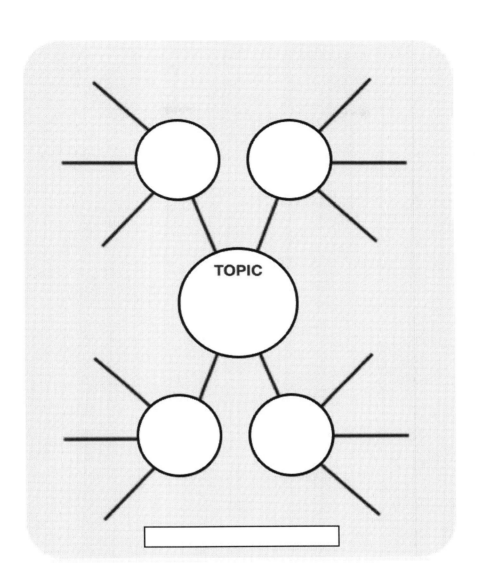

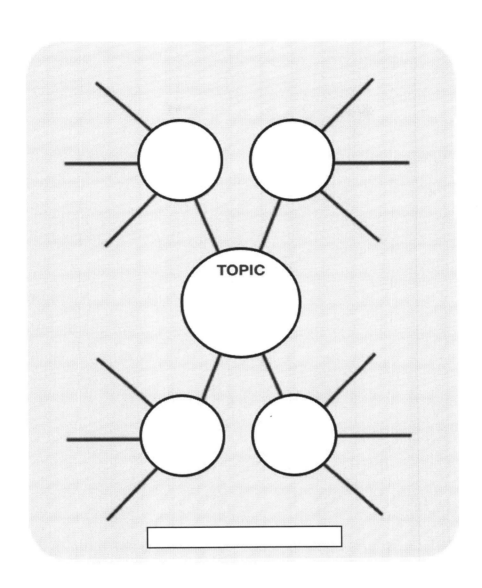

SERMON STARTER

DATE	
SEASON/EVENT	
SCRIPTURE	
TITLE/THEME	
KEY IDEA	
ILLUSTRATION	
ILLUSTRATION	
CONCLUDING STORY	
OTHER	

VALUES INDEX (circle the values highlighted in this message)

VOICE - ASSETS - LOVE - UNIQUENESS - EMPOWERMENT - SPIRITUALITY

changeyourministry.org

SERMON STARTER

DATE	
SEASON/EVENT	
SCRIPTURE	
TITLE/THEME	
KEY IDEA	
ILLUSTRATION	
ILLUSTRATION	
CONCLUDING STORY	
OTHER	

VALUES INDEX (circle the values highlighted in this message)

VOICE - ASSETS - LOVE - UNIQUENESS - EMPOWERMENT - SPIRITUALITY

changeyourministry.org

SERMON STARTER

DATE	
SEASON/EVENT	
SCRIPTURE	
TITLE/THEME	
KEY IDEA	
ILLUSTRATION	
ILLUSTRATION	
CONCLUDING STORY	
OTHER	

VALUES INDEX (circle the values highlighted in this message)

VOICE - ASSETS - LOVE - UNIQUENESS - EMPOWERMENT - SPIRITUALITY

changeyourministry.org

SERMON STARTER

DATE	
SEASON/EVENT	
SCRIPTURE	
TITLE/THEME	
KEY IDEA	
ILLUSTRATION	
ILLUSTRATION	
CONCLUDING STORY	
OTHER	

VALUES INDEX (circle the values highlighted in this message)

VOICE - ASSETS - LOVE - UNIQUENESS - EMPOWERMENT - SPIRITUALITY

changeyourministry.org

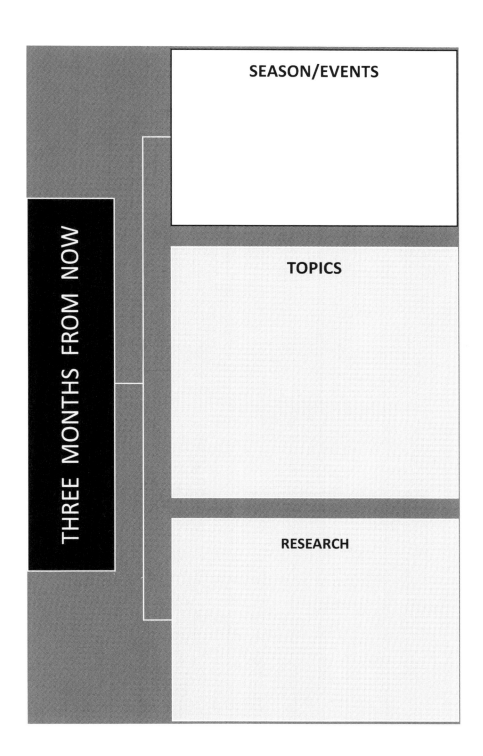

THREE MONTHS FROM NOW

SEASON/EVENTS

TOPICS

RESEARCH

SERMON STARTER

DATE	
SEASON/EVENT	
SCRIPTURE	
TITLE/THEME	
KEY IDEA	
ILLUSTRATION	
ILLUSTRATION	
CONCLUDING STORY	
OTHER	

VALUES INDEX (circle the values highlighted in this message)

VOICE - ASSETS - LOVE - UNIQUENESS - EMPOWERMENT - SPIRITUALITY

changeyourministry.org

SERMON STARTER

DATE	
SEASON/EVENT	
SCRIPTURE	
TITLE/THEME	
KEY IDEA	
ILLUSTRATION	
ILLUSTRATION	
CONCLUDING STORY	
OTHER	

VALUES INDEX (circle the values highlighted in this message)

VOICE - ASSETS - LOVE - UNIQUENESS - EMPOWERMENT - SPIRITUALITY

changeyourministry.org

SERMON STARTER

DATE	
SEASON/EVENT	
SCRIPTURE	
TITLE/THEME	
KEY IDEA	
ILLUSTRATION	
ILLUSTRATION	
CONCLUDING STORY	
OTHER	

VALUES INDEX (circle the values highlighted in this message)

VOICE - ASSETS - LOVE - UNIQUENESS - EMPOWERMENT - SPIRITUALITY

changeyourministry.org

SERMON STARTER

DATE	
SEASON/EVENT	
SCRIPTURE	
TITLE/THEME	
KEY IDEA	
ILLUSTRATION	
ILLUSTRATION	
CONCLUDING STORY	
OTHER	

VALUES INDEX (circle the values highlighted in this message)

VOICE - ASSETS - LOVE - UNIQUENESS - EMPOWERMENT - SPIRITUALITY

changeyourministry.org

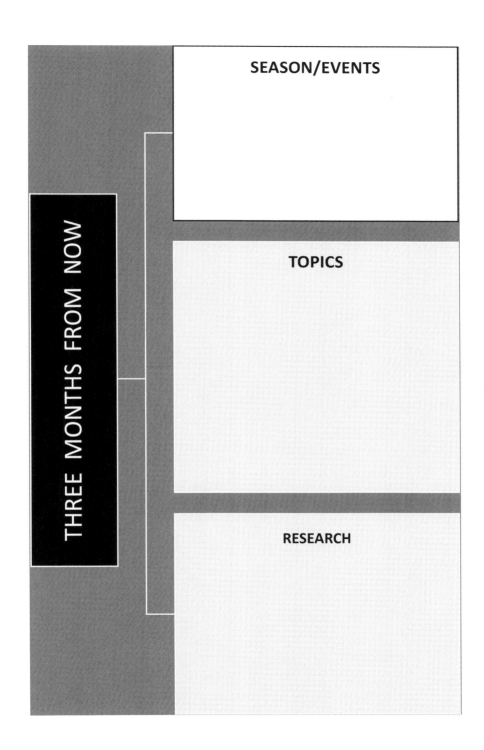

THREE MONTHS FROM NOW

SEASON/EVENTS

TOPICS

RESEARCH

SERMON STARTER

DATE	
SEASON/EVENT	
SCRIPTURE	
TITLE/THEME	
KEY IDEA	
ILLUSTRATION	
ILLUSTRATION	
CONCLUDING STORY	
OTHER	

VALUES INDEX (circle the values highlighted in this message)

VOICE - ASSETS - LOVE - UNIQUENESS - EMPOWERMENT - SPIRITUALITY

changeyourministry.org

SERMON STARTER

DATE	
SEASON/EVENT	
SCRIPTURE	
TITLE/THEME	
KEY IDEA	
ILLUSTRATION	
ILLUSTRATION	
CONCLUDING STORY	
OTHER	

VALUES INDEX (circle the values highlighted in this message)

VOICE - ASSETS - LOVE - UNIQUENESS - EMPOWERMENT - SPIRITUALITY

changeyourministry.org

SERMON STARTER

DATE	
SEASON/EVENT	
SCRIPTURE	
TITLE/THEME	
KEY IDEA	
ILLUSTRATION	
ILLUSTRATION	
CONCLUDING STORY	
OTHER	

VALUES INDEX (circle the values highlighted in this message)

VOICE - ASSETS - LOVE - UNIQUENESS - EMPOWERMENT - SPIRITUALITY

changeyourministry.org

SERMON STARTER

DATE	
SEASON/EVENT	
SCRIPTURE	
TITLE/THEME	
KEY IDEA	
ILLUSTRATION	
ILLUSTRATION	
CONCLUDING STORY	
OTHER	

VALUES INDEX (circle the values highlighted in this message)

VOICE - ASSETS - LOVE - UNIQUENESS - EMPOWERMENT - SPIRITUALITY

changeyourministry.org

SERMON STARTER

DATE	
SEASON/EVENT	
SCRIPTURE	
TITLE/THEME	
KEY IDEA	
ILLUSTRATION	
ILLUSTRATION	
CONCLUDING STORY	
OTHER	

VALUES INDEX (circle the values highlighted in this message)

VOICE - ASSETS - LOVE - UNIQUENESS - EMPOWERMENT - SPIRITUALITY

changeyourministry.org

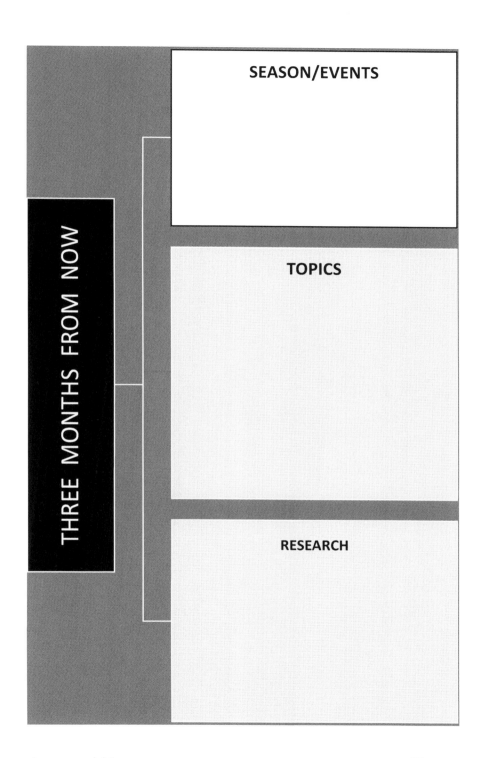

SEASON/EVENTS

THREE MONTHS FROM NOW

TOPICS

RESEARCH

NOTES

NOTES

NOTES

NOTES

NOTES

NOTES

CHANGE YOUR MINISTRY
being Church in a Culture of Change
changeyourministry.org

Go to www.changeyourministry.org and Amazon.com for these resources.

The *Change Your Ministry Leader's Assessment* is designed to help leaders discover their passion for ministry. Plan to have an assessment for each participant in your training. Use it with the *Change Your Ministry Leader's Assessment Seminar Guidebook* and you will have a powerful set of materials to empower your leadership. The guidebook includes four sessions and a password to access presentation slides, notes, and templates at changeyourministry.org.

The *Change Your Ministry Preacher's Journal 1, 2, 3, & 4* provides an innovative system to create and manage your sermons for the whole year. Each journal contains material for a quarter of the year.

Contact Craig Kennet Miller at cmiller@changeyourministry.org
for consultations, seminars, and teaching.

Made in the USA
Middletown, DE
01 June 2019